KODAK SAFETY FILM 5077
KODAK SAFETY FILM
KODAK SAFETY FILM 5036

£ 1·75

KENNY EVERETT'S

VIDEO SHOW

Annual 1980

CONTENTS

Stafford Pemberton Publishing

Based on the Cosgrove Hall production Captain Kremmen

Published in Great Britain by Stafford Pemberton.
Publishing Co. Ltd.,
The Ruskin Chambers, Drury Lane, Knutsford,
Cheshire WA16 6HA.
Printed and bound in Italy
ISBN 0 86030 199 0

I FORBID YOU TO THROW THAT PIE
F.U.S

BOTTLE JOB IN FREAK CITY
THE KROAKUM MEDICAL CENTRE, FREAK CITY, EARTH. I, CAPTAIN KREMMEN, HAD JUST UNDERGONE AN EXHAUSTIVE CHECK UP IN THE HANDS OF DR. IDWAL SMITH, INVENTOR OF THE TWO-WHEELED OVERCOAT AND PIONEER OF THE ILLUMINATED BRAILLE PUZZLE BOOK FOR UNBORN CHILDREN. THE REASON? I WAS ABOUT TO START ON A PERILOUS MISSION..
WHAT IS IT DOC? YOU LOOK SO WORRIED.
WITH GOOD REASON CAPTAIN. EITHER YOU'VE GOT A HOLE IN THE HEART OR - I'LL GIVE IT TO YOU STRAIGHT - YOU'VE GOT A POLO MINT IN THE POCKET OF YOUR PYJAMAS.
I SUCKED RUMINATIVELY ON THE AFORESAID MORSEL.
IT'S TOUGH- VERY TOUGH.
WELL DON'T TRY TO CHEW IT, CAPTAIN.
LISTEN - THE SUPER-ADVANCED NATIVES OF THARGOIDIA ARE RESTLESS. ANY MOMENT NOW THEY WILL TRY AND ATTACK EARTH - WE MUST PACIFY THEM.
O.K. I'LL GET THE MIRRORS AND BEADS -AND A BIG STICK.
SOON WE WERE HEADING SPACEWARDS IN TRUSTY TROLL ONE.
ARE THE THARGOIDS VERY INTELLIGENT CAPTAIN?
VERY- THEIR LIFT OPERATORS ARE ISSUED WITH LONG THIN MAPS INCORPORATING TWO ARROWS - HIGH CHOLESTEROL IS A PUBLIC HOLIDAY - MIND READERS CHARGE HALF PRICE AND.....
CAPTAIN! THERE'S SOMETHING OUTSIDE!

CARLA WAS RIGHT! SUDDENLY THE THREE OF US WERE CAUGHT BY SOME STRANGE POWER, FROZEN IN TIME BY PARALYTIC EMANATIONS FROM THE ENEMY VESSEL...
COMPLETELY PARALYSED, I WATCHED HELPLESSLY AS THE ALIENS BOARDED TROLL ONE WITHOUT OPPOSITION...
AHA! CAPTAIN KREMMEN THE GREAT SUPER HERO. ALLOW ME TO INTRODUCE MYSELF, I AM CAPTAIN CATAPULT OF THE THARGOIDIAN SPACEFLEET AND THIS IS MY BOSON... ARROWS - PREPARE TO DIE!
DIE? I REMEMBERED MY DOCTOR'S WARNING ABOUT MY LOW THRESHHOLD OF DEATH... WITH A SUPREME EFFORT I BATTED AN EYELID.
IF ONLY....
THE EYELID MOVED! ENCOURAGED, I SUMMONED ALL MY CONSIDERABLE WILL POWER TO REPEAT THE ACT... CAUSING AN UPDRAFT OVER MY BREAST POCKET!
IT'S COMING!
AND CAUSING MY SIGNED PHOTOGRAPH OF NICHOLAS PARSONS TO RISE FROM MY BREAST POCKET...
MY AWARD WINNING COURAGE PAID OFF...
DONE IT!
AS THEIR EYES LIT UPON THE LIKENESS THE ALIENS WERE STRUCK BY THE BLIBBERING HEEBY JEEBIES AND THE PARALYSING POWER WAS RELEASED.
QUICK CARLA, FLUSH THEM DOWN THE SPACE HATCH AND WE CAN ESCAPE.
BLIBBER BLIBBERERBER
BUT EVEN AS ONE VILE SMELLING MENACE WAS FLUSHED INTO OBSCURITY - ANOTHER APPEARED...
CAPTAIN! THERE'S SOMETHING ELSE! LOOK!
GOTTERDAMMERUNG! IT'S HEADING STRAIGHT FOR US!. MEIN GOTT. IT'S.. IT'S....
A PUTRON BOMB! GET THE CLOTHES PEGS!

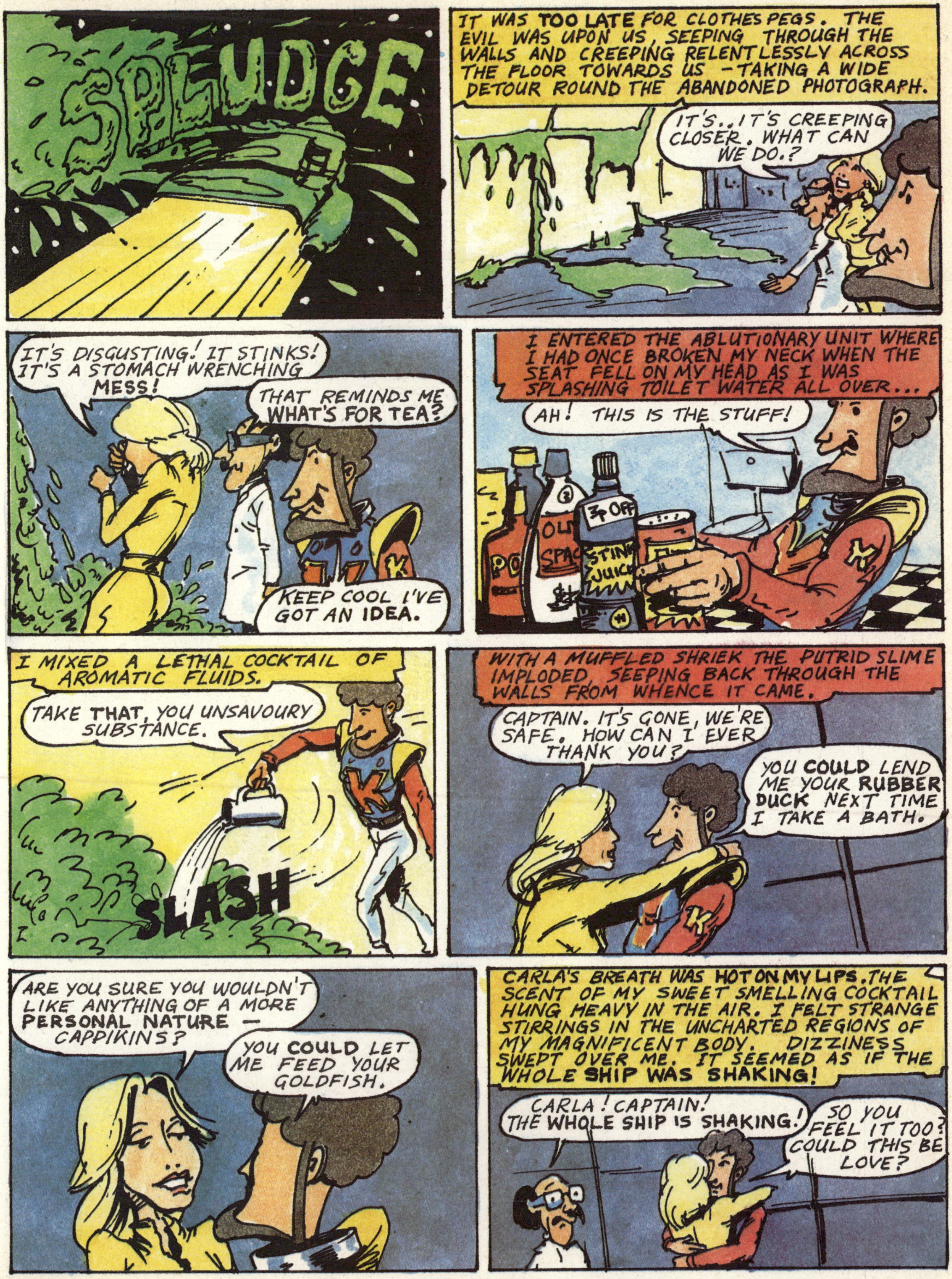
SPLUDGE
IT WAS TOO LATE FOR CLOTHES PEGS. THE EVIL WAS UPON US, SEEPING THROUGH THE WALLS AND CREEPING RELENTLESSLY ACROSS THE FLOOR TOWARDS US — TAKING A WIDE DETOUR ROUND THE ABANDONED PHOTOGRAPH.
IT'S.. IT'S CREEPING CLOSER. WHAT CAN WE DO.?
IT'S DISGUSTING! IT STINKS! IT'S A STOMACH WRENCHING MESS!
THAT REMINDS ME WHAT'S FOR TEA?
KEEP COOL I'VE GOT AN IDEA.
I ENTERED THE ABLUTIONARY UNIT WHERE I HAD ONCE BROKEN MY NECK WHEN THE SEAT FELL ON MY HEAD AS I WAS SPLASHING TOILET WATER ALL OVER...
AH! THIS IS THE STUFF!
I MIXED A LETHAL COCKTAIL OF AROMATIC FLUIDS.
TAKE THAT, YOU UNSAVOURY SUBSTANCE.
SLASH
WITH A MUFFLED SHRIEK THE PUTRID SLIME IMPLODED, SEEPING BACK THROUGH THE WALLS FROM WHENCE IT CAME.
CAPTAIN. IT'S GONE, WE'RE SAFE. HOW CAN I EVER THANK YOU?
YOU COULD LEND ME YOUR RUBBER DUCK NEXT TIME I TAKE A BATH.
ARE YOU SURE YOU WOULDN'T LIKE ANYTHING OF A MORE PERSONAL NATURE — CAPPIKINS?
YOU COULD LET ME FEED YOUR GOLDFISH.
CARLA'S BREATH WAS HOT ON MY LIPS. THE SCENT OF MY SWEET SMELLING COCKTAIL HUNG HEAVY IN THE AIR. I FELT STRANGE STIRRINGS IN THE UNCHARTED REGIONS OF MY MAGNIFICENT BODY. DIZZINESS SWEPT OVER ME. IT SEEMED AS IF THE WHOLE SHIP WAS SHAKING!
CARLA! CAPTAIN! THE WHOLE SHIP IS SHAKING!
SO YOU FEEL IT TOO? COULD THIS BE LOVE?

FAR FROM IT CAPTAIN. WE ARE IN THE GRIP OF A MYSTERIOUS TRACTOR BEAM - AND IT'S PULLING US STRAIGHT TOWARDS THAT PLANET.
GOOD HEAVENS! THARGOIDIA!
THARGOIDIA
THE TRACTOR BEAM DREW US RELENTLESSLY DOWN TOWARDS THE PLANET'S SURFACE....
WE'RE GOING TO CRASH!
HAVE FAITH, CARLA. I'M GOING TO TRY ONE OF MY FAMOUS SOFT LANDING
BLANG
AKKA
lkrtinkle
BEFORE WE HAD TIME TO RECOVER WE WERE OVERWHELMED BY HEAVILY ARMED THARGOID GUARDS.
ON YOUR FEET EARTHLINGS! GORT WANTS TO SEE YOU.
GORT! THE FACE THAT FRIED A THOUSAND CHIPS. A BEING OF SUCH AWESOME POWER THAT EVERY TIME HE BLEW HIS NOSE THEY RAISE TOWER-BRIDGE.
A MEGLOMANIAC SO VAIN THAT EVEN THE BAGS UNDER HIS EYES HAD HIS INITIALS ON.
SUCH WAS THE STRENGTH OF OUR ENEMY.....
OUR PRISON POD SPED ALONG THE MONORAIL ABOVE THARGOIDIA'S STRANGELY BEAUTIFUL CAPITAL....
'..... FINALLY STOPPING AT GORT'S MAGNIFICENT PALACE.
WOW! DO YOU REALLY THINK IT'S MADE OF SOLID DIAMOND?
IF IT ISN'T HE WAS CHEATED OUT OF THE 10p IT COST HIM!
SILENCE YOU SCUMMY LITTLE TWERPS.
PREPARE TO MEET GORT. ENTER ON YOUR KNEES.

ON MY KNEES? ME? CAPTAIN KREMMEN, GUARDIAN OF THE FREE WORLD, THIGHS LIKE TUG BOATS, MUSCLES OF STEEL, HEART OF OAK, VEST OF....
ON YOUR KNEES OR WITHOUT EYEBALLS
THE CLIMB TO GORT'S THRONE-ROOM WAS SLOW....
COME IN YOU INSIGNIFICANT PILES OF UNSAVOURY GARBAGE.
SO YOU THOUGHT YOU COULD FOIL MY PLAN TO EXECUTE THE ENTIRE POPULATION OF EARTH AND THEN STEAL THE MONEY FROM THEIR GAS METERS? YOU BRAINLESS, PITIFUL, IDIOTIC NONENTITIES. I GORT, AM INVINCIBLE!
YOU FIEND! YOU'LL NEVER GET AWAY WITH IT
BUT I WILL! AND WITH ALL THAT MONEY I CAN AFFORD A NEW BRIDGE FOR MY TRAIN SET. GUARDS TAKE THEM AWAY TO SOONARU 9!
SOONARU 9, A THARGOID MOON MADE ENTIRELY OF RADIO ACTIVE MUD WHERE MINDLESS SHELLS OF HUMANITY TOILED TO MINE THE MUD TO FEED THE THARGOID ENERGY FURNACES....
YOU KNOW, DON'T YOU CAPTAIN, THAT THE RADIO-ACTIVE MUD WILL EVENTUALLY ROT OUR BRAINS.
FOR SOMEONE WHOSE BRAIN ONCE EXPLODED AND DIDN'T EVEN RUFFLE HIS HAIR, YOU WORRY A LOT, OLD FRIEND.
THE FUEL WAS CALCULATED TO RUN-OUT ONCE INSIDE SOONARU 9'S MAGNETIC PULL.
Phut
phut
BARP
EXCUSE ME!
SOONARU 9
PSSSSIIIIIIEEEUUU

BLETCH!
WE CLIMBED FROM THE PRISON-SHIP TO BE MET BY A FEARSOME SIGHT.
UGH! WHATS THAT?
ONE OF THE MUDMEN, FOR SOMEONE WITH SIX ELBOWS AND EYEBROWS WHICH MEET IN THE MIDDLE OF HIS BACK - HE'S NOT BAD LOOKING IN AN UGLY SORT OF WAY.
THE MUDMAN OPENED A HOLE IN HIS HEAD....
DUH-DUH, DUH-DUH
CAPTAIN, I THINK HE'S TRYING TO TELL US SOMETHING.
WHAT'S HE SAYING?
DUH-DUH-DUH
I DON'T KNOW MAYBE HE'S TRYING TO HELP US.
COME ON MAN-SPIT IT OUT!
SLAT
HE WAS SAYING THAT IT'S AWFULLY HARD TO TALK WITH A MOUTHFUL OF MUD!
CAPTAIN OH CAPTAIN- WE'RE MAROONED ON A HOSTILE PLANET, EARTH IS ABOUT TO BE DESTROYED, GORT IS ABOUT TO CONQUER THE UNIVERSE - AND I'VE NOT FILED MY NAILS FOR MORE THAN A WEEK WHAT ARE WE GOING TO DO?
WHAT INDEED? MUD GILBERTS EVERYWHERE - EARTH IN PERIL AND ALREADY RADIOACTIVE MUD IS TAKING ITS TOLL ON MY CREW, CAN WE SURVIVE - FIND OUT SHORTLY IN THE CURSE OF THE RAMPAGING UNDERPANTS

Yes, it's the most glittering night on the Cosmic Calendar, when celestial celebrities from all over the universe come to witness the amazing conglomeration of laughter, beauty and talent. It's the

COSMI-VISION JOKE TELLING BEAUTY CONTEST

And here to present the show is that unctuous crawler with the frog's legs – The man who's always sincere whether he means it or not – Dago Slasher Distemper!

"Hello fans! Lovable little me here and what a show I've got for you! Our six beautiful finalists have already demonstrated one unique aspect of their multiple talents and now, in the final round of our competition, our gorgeous contestants have to show off their bodies and tell us a joke. So, without further ado, let's meet our first contestant.

Tworg sets the show going in magnificent style. This bouncy little creature with the forest of eyes waving on stalks on the end of her toes astounded us in the previous heat with her amazing telepathic chess match with a submerged radish. Take it away Tworg!"

"Thank you. There was this humanoid who had a friend who was the keeper at the zoo. One day the friend went to see the zoo-keeper and found him weeping on his knees by the body of a dead elephant. 'Is he . . .?' asked the friend. 'Yes,' said the keeper, 'he passed away this morning.' The friend put his hand on the keeper's shoulder. 'Such a noble beast,' he said, 'so strong and gentle – you must have loved him very much.' 'I did,' replied the keeper, 'but it's not that - it's me thats got to bury him.'"

"Thank you. Before I start I must admit that I am not a full blooded Zoolian – I'm two pints short. My joke concerns a young mother whose teenage daughter is forever using slang words, often repeating them so much her mother is driven to fury. One day the mum had had enough and she told her daughter so. 'I'm fed up of your slang,' she said angrily there's two words you keep on using over and over again. One is 'magic' and the other one is 'cruddy'. The daughter looked at her mother. 'Tell me what the cruddy one is and I'll try to cut it out."

"Me that's got to bury him! Haw haw haw Tworg, that will set them rolling in the aisles on your home planet of Sticklebania. Now let's have another big round of applause for our next contestant, that giant crustacean who in the preliminary heats showed us how chewing gum can stop your ears popping, then found she couldn't get it out – that full bodied, full bloodied Zoolian – Iki!"

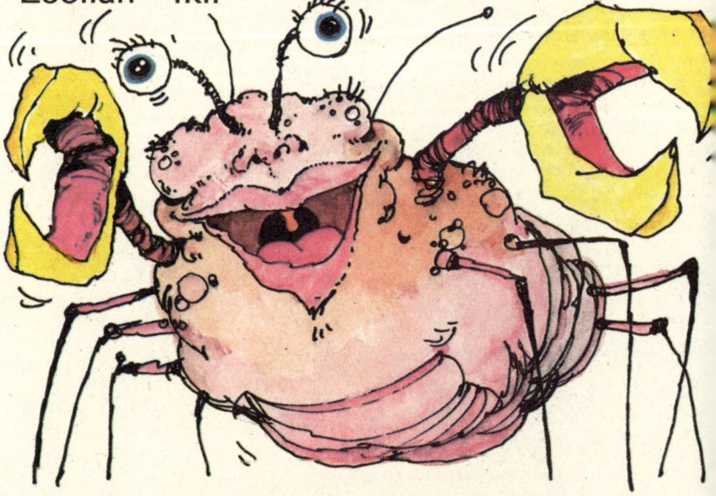

"Tee hee hee! What a corker! Thank you tremendously Iki. Next we have a beautiful mass of undulating porridge who showed us how to act our age and our shoe size at the same time – let's have more clapping for that lovable Plutowegian – Yach!"

"There was once an alien being who came down to earth and lived with a schoolteacher in Hebdon Bridge. He questioned the teacher constantly about the habits of the earth people and the different customs of different nations on earth. Eventually the talk came down to sport. 'Each country has its own national sport.' said the teacher. 'Really,' asked the alien, 'what is the different national sports of, say, Spain and England?' 'Well,' said the teacher, 'In Spain it's bull fighting and in England it's cricket.' 'Hmm,' said the alien, 'I think I'd prefer to fight crickets.'"

"Hoo hoo hoo! You're a proper caution and no mistake! Next we have that wonderful favourite from earth itself, who enthralled us previously when she played that haunting piece of music she had composed for dieters everywhere, 'Refrain from this and that'. Yes it's our very own Miss Raquel Whoppers! 'Raaaaaay!"

"Beat it, creep. Psshew! What a dummy that man is! I like my men with a bit more ooomph! If you know what I mean. Like this girlfriend I have, she used to go out with this gorgeous hunk of beefcake called Joe. They got engaged, but eventually she broke it off, which was a painful experience to both of them. Anyway, she still wanted to keep in touch so she wrote to him and asked if he would send her photograph back. Next day in the post he sent her 60 photographs and asked her to pick hers out."

"Snigger! Nice one Raquel. Our next contestant is that wonderful pile of telepathic rocks who showed us in the last round that if you laid all the worms in England in a line, one of them is bound to wriggle and spoil it all. As you know, Emelda Bleah from Mentaluna cannot speak, so she'll be projecting her joke to you through the incredible powers of telepathic transmission."

"Thank you, thank you, thank you so much. My story is about two cowboys playing cards. One of them is a rough, tough Westerner and the other is a dandy from back East. The Westerner keeps winning, until one game, when the pot in the middle grows bigger and bigger. At last the two players have to show their hands. The dandy lays down four aces. 'At last!' he cried excitedly, reaching for the money. The Westerner stops him with a look. 'Fraid not, partner, I just beat that.' 'What? You can't beat four aces! What have you got?' 'Two 45s and a bowie knife.' 'How come you're so lucky?"

"Pointed humour from Emelda there! Our last contestant showed us how she composes sheet music while still in bed. How good is she at rib-ticklers? Find out for yourself and give a really big hand to Sweet Fanny Arkwright from Tapt!"

"How droll. Now it is time for me to open the envelope that will tell us all who is the winner of this years Comi-Vision Joke Telling Beauty Contest, where marks are awarded for humour, ability and looks. Now let's just get this card out . . . And the winner is . . . Dago Slasher Distemper!"

". . . Sob! . . . Oh no, I can't believe it! Not after last year, and the year before, and the year before that! Sob! It's incredible! Even I am not that fantastic! . . . But you the viewers know best so thank you from the bottom of my heart. Thank you! This is the happiest day of my life! Thank you thank you thank you . . . I love you all . . . I never thought . . . Thank you . . . sob . . ."

They said it could never happen again!
The evil menace returns!

Normality is not Dead

Yes, this frightening news of the ressurection of the world's most evil and obscure cult, Normality, will shock and outrage thousands of people throughout the world. The rise of the bizarre hocus pocus of sensible shoes, suits and well groomed hair will strike terror into the hearts of all of us who thought the world had rid itself of this extremist threat once and for all.

Not so. For years, small pockets of normal people have been existing inside their homes, watching television, playing with their cats, having tea in the afternoon. Now these people are ready to rise. The years of waiting and planning are finally over. Already, there are signs that Normality's heinous by-product, work, is infecting the minds and lives of thousands of people who would otherwise be living respectable abnormal lives. One daring undercover agent, posing as a debt collector for a T.V. rental firm penetrated this close knit sub-culture and lived to tell the tale. Here he pinpoints some of the things to watch out for, if we are to combat the astonishing upsurge in Normality.

Despite an elaborate defensive network of smiles, handshakes, winks and nods, cult devotees often give themselves away in a number of ways.

1. Normal people never crawl around on all fours, barking loudly.
2. Normal people never blow their noses on their ties.
3. Normal people often watch football on television.
4. Normal people never have 'cut here' tattooed on their throats.
5. Normal people walk by putting one leg in front of the other.

It seemed like a nightmare, but it was true! I hoped against hope I was dreaming, but I knew deep down it was only too real – horribly, frighteningly real! An overload in the Thrustal Boosters had sent me spinning through the Space-Time continuum into the nether world beyond. I had passed through a rip in the very fabric of space itself and now I was trapped, caught in limbo, marooned on that most barren and desolate place. Gonzoville, the planet of old jokes. Yes, I had come down in Gonzoville, the sleazy underbelly of a space ghetto where derelict jokes eked out the last pitiful days of their existence. In a place where the strongest minds crumble and warp at ½ entendres from a closed mind, even I Captain Kremmen did not realise how close I was to a

Psych-Out In Gonzoville!

How wrong I was. Before I knew it I was lost in a crowd of ex Prime Ministers gesticulating wildly into mirrors and thumping hollow wooden tubs with their fists. Next to them a legion of po-faced sports commentators sat mouthing incoherently as they reported the progress of two flies in a sugar bowl. I stopped and tried to pull myself together. I had to escape. I couldn't let it end here. I had to escape, but how?

I stepped down from Troll 1 to be met by huge tannoy blaring out the one about the Englishman, the Irishman and the Scotsman. To my left a narrow street stretched into the distance, with a man knocking on every door and a voice from inside saying "who's there?" I hurried off in the opposite direction, shielding my eyes from an ants vs. elephants football game. I stopped briefly to let a chicken cross the road and then pressed on past a vat of shark infested custard, stopping only to say 'sir' to a gorilla with a machine gun. More tannoys appeared, asking me the difference between a jailer and a jeweller, so I put my fingers to my ears and ran. Surely things couldn't get any worse.

I stopped and watched a group of talk show hosts pulling faces at each other and skirted a circle of stand-up comics who were peering over each others shoulders and scribbling jokes about kick starting Jumbo Jets. A large crowd of Mothers-in-Law stood menacingly by, their umbrellas raised. The hair on the back of my neck prickled with fear as a thousand t.v. detectives in grubby raincoats approached me whispering "Hmmmm Betty!" and "Who loves ya, baby?" I shuddered as I passed the entire cast of Crossroads squabbling over a good line, and I winced with pity when Captain Kirk came up and begged me for 2p so he could meekly go where everyone else does. I felt my reason slipping away and I fought to regain control of my mind. To think that I, Captain Kremmen, the world's most fabulous man, was trapped in this insane graveyard. My steely self control forced me not to think of the real world beyond. I would rather have fought a thousand Venusian Schlurpers than stay here another second longer.

I ran. I couldn't think what else to do. I closed my eyes, put my head down and ran and ran and ran. I don't know how long I ran for – days – maybe months – but eventually I came to a sobbing halt and looked around me.

The landscape had altered drastically. I was on a narrow, rocky trail, shrouded in thick mist. The trail led upwards. I racked my brains. Somewhere in my memory a faint strip stirring began. I had heard of this place before, but I had dismissed the story as a bar-room showpiece for travellers who'd had too much rocket fuel in their coffee. Now I knew it was true. I was nearing the Legendary Home of The Ancient Ones, the almost mythical hideout where old jokes limped off to die. I gritted my teeth and pressed forward.

The mist grew thicker as I stepped over the crumbling bones of long dead jokes. Perhaps some of the Ancient Ones might still be alive. The silence was immense, deafening, but chill fingers ran up and down my spine as some eerie sixth sense told me I was not alone. I hid behind a rock, peered into the mist and listened.

Yes, there was something alive. Something was moving ahead of me.

"Why DID the little chicken cross the road, damn you!" A voice cried. "Tell me you fake – tell me!"

At once everything became clear. I recognised the voice as that of a man who has enslaved an entire nation through soundwaves alone, a voice so powerful that to travel through the very fabric of time and space to get new material would be a mere formality. I watched the powerful hands grip tighter on the throat.

He turned suddenly, his oriental eyes ablaze, a snarl disfiguring his baby face.

For hours the figure wandered among the dusty relics of a bygone age. And then a slight noise sounded and the figure tensed, his eyes bright, his teeth gleaming through the mist. As silently as a Martian cat, he turned, and without warning, sprang upon one of the Ancient Ones, gripping it firmly by the throat and shaking it vigorously, in the manner a rabid dog shakes a rat.

"Tony, it's me – Captain Kremmen."

He dropped the lifeless body to the floor and his face cracked open into a smile and he stuffed a thick notebook into his trouser pocket.

"Captain Kremmen, of course. Glad to see you. Welcome to the show. Can I give you a lift back to earth? Have I told you the one about –"

We picked up Troll 1 and returned to earth.

Everedy Video News

M.P. Lashes out at 'Scandalmongers'

The Right-Honourable Digweed Thrimble described allegations that he was about to resign following an incident concerning a top jockey, a showgirl, a large plate of spaghetti and a jigsaw as "Bilge. Utter tosh."

Mr. Thrimble, speaking from inside a drawer in his office said: "I know nothing about this incident, or even if such an incident took place. In fact I know nothing at all about anything and never have. I have done nothing to be ashamed of. I have done nothing at all in my twenty years in politics and my record will bear me out on this point."

After lashing out at 'scandalmongering' in the press, Mr. Thrimble said: "As far as the alleged incident is concerned I never did it and I promise I won't do it again."

Union boss calls for all-out strike

Union leader Wally Wombat urged his men to take all out strike action after a pay row at their London depot. "We brothers have got to stand together." He said. "The committee is quite firm on this point. They have promised to stand behind me and I shall be standing behind them."

The dispute is over the wages received by Melvin Stopcockle who works as a light switcher onner at the factory. Last week his wages were 2p short. "It's daylight robbery," said Mr. Wombat. "These vampires are sucking our life-blood and giving it to faceless men behind big desks who haven't done a day's work in their lives and live off the back of the workers grinding their faces into the ground."

A spokesman for the firm's management pointed out that the previous week Mr. Stopcockle had received £50 extra in his wages and made no protest then. "That's just what I'm getting at," said Mr. Wombat. "This management is inefficient. We can overlook one mistake, but after two in two weeks we have to make a protest."

Minister Lashes 'Judas' Britain

Cabinet Minister Egwell Dunne yesterday launched a bitter attack on Britons who are ready to sell 'our national heritage' to the highest bidder. Speaking at the Commission For Bombastic Imbeciles annual dinner-dance he said: "Stately homes, national monuments, artistic treasures, fish and chip shops - they're all being sold for a pittance. We're selling our birthright for a mess of pottage just like Judas!

Adding that Britain would 'rue the day' he cited a recent case where a wealthy Arab brought his three sons to Britain for a holiday. The Arab asked the eldest son what he would like as a going home present. The boy said a boat, so the Arab bought him the QE2. The second son wanted a plane so the Arab bought him a Concorde. The third son asked for a cowboy outfit so the Arab bought him the Department of Inland Revenue.

"We've got to get back to basics." said Mr. Dunne. "We've got to keep our chins and stiffen those upper lips."

DID YOU KNOW

In 1916 Private Godfrey Noble defeated an entire regiment of German tanks using only a piece of string.

Inside:

I married a Walrus from Mars!
Off-Stage Antics
Aunty Carla's problem page.

Plus:

Free Money!
Real Girls!

And:

Gardening hints.
Pet's corner.
Plus our usual round up of news and views.

Sport - The Gibber Hits Out.
Rumpus at Aintree.

Adventure: I survived the mad doctor.
Romance: Part 3 of our serial One Tender Summer.

PET POURRI
with Freddie Feedham.

Regular readers of this column will be well aware of my research into communications between man and beast. Through long painstaking hours I have developed a rudimentary 'Language' consisting of grunts and signs that my cat Rudolph can both understand and use himself. We have spent many long hours in pleasant conversation and he has proved to be both lucid and intelligent. But just how intelligent is he? Are felines really our mental equals? I shall relate the happenings of last Saturday and you may draw your own conclusions.

We were sitting in the living room drinking cocoa and watching the world match play tiddleywink competition on the television when Rudolph remarked that cats had a much better developed sixth sense than humans. He claimed they were able to forsee the future better. Immediately I took up the challenge and asked him who would wink the winning tiddle of the match in progress. He plumped for Joe Green and I tipped Tommy Turquoise, with £5 wagered on the result. Anyway Tommy duly obliged and Rudolph was forced to cough up. I put the note behind the clock on the mantlepiece and told him that I would have it framed as proof of the day mankind finally showed itself to be cleverer than cats.

"In that case," he replied getting out a pen, "Give it back to me and I'll write you a cheque."

OFF STAGE ANTICS
By Nona Ames-Packdrill, the friend of the famous.

The behaviour of diminutive Judge Justice Chief Nigel Noserag – one of those small things sent to try us – continues to cause concern among his colleagues. Yesterday, while deliberating on Marcio Malevolent's claim that he was only trying to cure his wife's hiccups when the axe slipped, a fire engine went past the court, sirens wailing. The judge leapt up, shouted 'Stop!' and ran from the courtroom, only to return a few minutes later claiming he hadn't really wanted an ice lolly anyway.

An amusing tale has come to my notice concerning You-Know-Who's best friend, bi-sexual disco graffitti artist Velda Brickrifle. Velda, unusually tired and emotional, was at the fancy dress bash at Benn's held to launch Sarah, Duke of Cuckooland, in her new career as a part time social worker. Asked by a mutual friend if Sarah and she were related, Velda snorted and said, "The girl's a pea-brained nincompoop with large feet." "That *Could* be coincidence." answered the friend, city financier Hugo Gelt.

Alas, the manual dexterity of ace guitarist Terry Twang does not extend past the fretboard. While taking champagne and strawberries at Terry's Mayfair home, he regaled me with stories of his prowess at carpentry, boasting how he had decorated the flat himself and built several of the articles of furniture. Hardly had the words left his lips when the clock struck, the cuckoo backed out, scratched his head and asked what time it was.

HOW on earth did punk rock star Biff Thud smuggle a live mongoose into the Sleezo Cabaret just as Vera Wobbly and her Naughty Snake were beginning their act?

WHICH famous actress, promised subdued lighting and romantic atmosphere in a sea food restaurant by a well known Lothario found herself in the chip shop wearing dark glasses?

WHY are you reading this piffle?

MY HUSBAND WAS A MARTIAN WALRUS?
by Norma Le Housewife.

Astounding! Amazing! Incredible!

Yes, I married a walrus from Mars. Well, I didn't actually, but that's what I thought had happened one night after I'd been to a wine tasting class at college and (Continued on page 7.)

Hey, Stupid!

Yes, YOU, dummy! What do you mean you're not stupid? You're reading this aren't you? But don't worry some of the most intelligent people in the world are stupid, just like you. Stupidity doesn't bear the same social stigma it used to and that is partly the result of *Amazing New Surgical Technique* that can remove all traces of stupidity from your face. That inane grin will be transformed into a cheery smile, that silly look will become a studious air. Send Now for details. P.O. Box 222.

She was young and beautiful; he was strong and manly. They met . . .

One Tender Summer

The story so far: Alison Faynesworth, after escaping from an orphanage with the help of Vito, a handsome gypsy horse dealer, finally finds acceptance in London's high society with her charming puppet show. While performing one night she is attacked by her doctor and falls through the stage trapdoor into the Thames and is saved from death by Peter, a trapeze artist who has the plague. After handing her a snuff box containing six tiny plastic hands he is killed by a Jack Russell wearing horn rimmed spectacles. Fleeing into a darkened tunnel she is led to a door by a life size model of David Hamilton. As she moves to open the door the hideous dwarf leaps up and embraces her. Now read on . . .

"Darling," gasped the slavering midget, "Your face is all hairy!"

"Get off my back," replied Alison, freeing the podgy hands from her neck and hurling the misshapen troll into the darkness. There was a faint splash and then a faint cry.

"Don't you want to make any dedications?"

Alison shrugged and pushed at the thick wooden door. Slowly and soundlessly it swung inward to reveal a dimly lit room with one table, where a handsome clean featured man sat polishing a tortoise. Alison caught her breath at the sight of his thin aquiline nose, his clear blue eyes and his sensuous, slightly arrogant mouth. Her heart thumped against her chest and she flushed noisily. Where had she seen those features before? Was it Count Dimitri? Sir Henry? She searched her mind, sure that this magnificent specimen was someone she had met before. Was it Count Rupert? Baron Olaf? Prince Max? Or was it the woman who cleaned the drains at the orphanage?

Suddenly the time for speculation had gone. The man rose to his feet, bowed slightly and offered Alison a seat. She took it and sat gazing across the table into his sad blue eyes that seemed to ache with love. He reached behind his ear and handed her a card. It was the queen of hearts, and someone had drawn a pair of spectacles and a beard onto the monarch's face. As Alison studied the mysterious gift a fly started buzzing some ten feet behind her head.

Immediately the man stiffened, his eyes wide, his muscles tense, his senses alert. Without a sound he opened his mouth and with terrifying speed his monstrous tongue flew through the air, unravelling itself as it did so. It flew over Alison's shoulder, snatched up the fly and then flew back into the man's mouth. He sat there smiling as though nothing had happened.

Although the incident had taken a fraction of a second, Alison was shocked and a little frightened. Her hopes of rescuing her father and proving that she was the rightful queen of Rusticania seemed further than ever from success. She might never star in a major Hollywood production. She suppressed a sob and clutched her hands to her chest as hot tears of confusion welled in her eyes.

Yes, Alison was frightened and confused, but it was not the sight of the fleshy protruberence whistling wetly past her ear that frightened her. It was not the smirk on the man's face that confused her. What disturbed Alison was the strange, mystical word she had seen tattooed on the slimy underside of that monstrous tongue. A word with no obvious meaning, but ringing with magic demons from inhuman, ungodly worlds.

SINGALONGAMAX

What did it mean?

To be continued.

DID YOU KNOW?

Fifi Lamont, an American housewife, can spot a blonde hair on her husband's coat at a distance of seventy miles, but has never yet driven her car into the garage without crashing.

Aunty Carla's problem spot

Dear Aunty Carla,
While I was courting my wife, her father kept saying that the man who landed his daughter would get a prize. We have been married two months and I still haven't received it. Is this fair?

Dear Disgruntled,
A man can put his foot down before he's married, but afterwards he hasn't got a leg to stand on.

Dear Aunty Carla,
When I asked my boyfriend if he thought we should get married, he burst out laughing. I pressed him on the subject he became very irritable and offensive. When I went down on one knee and begged him to marry me he grabbed me by the scruff of the neck and hurled me through the back door. Do you think he might not love me?
Yours in suspense,
Wimpy

Dear Wimpy,
Of course he loves you! Now he's got that little lot out of his system I'm sure he'll be only too willing to name the day.

Dear Aunty Carla,
It was our silver wedding anniversary last week and my husband came home with a bottle of wine. Later on in the evening he forced himself on me and demanded that I kissed him. Is there something wrong with him?
Yours disgustedly,
Worried.

Dear Worried,
Sadly, there is nothing you can do about this lecherous kind of behaviour. Just consider yourself lucky that you'll only have to go through it once every twenty-five years.

Dear Aunty Carla,
When I remarried I told my wife to treat my house as her own. Since then she has been holding wild parties every day. Is this fair?
Yours in hindsight,
Unhappy

Dear Unhappy,
Of course it's fair. Consider yourself lucky she hasn't sold it.

More next issue. . . . .

BALD?

Forget it. New Tufty-Top Spray on hair will cure baldness *Permanently*. All you need is a bucket full of hair (small strips of plastic or paper will do) and one can of New Tufty-Top Spray on Locks. To increase your hairier area just spray the head with Tufty-Top super adhesive and then dip it into the bucket. Far out! You're young again!
Warning: Please follow the instructions carefully.

DID YOU KNOW?
When singing in Rome after a large meal of spaghetti, famous Italian tenor Luigi Bellosi sneezed and lassoed the first three rows of the audience.

DID YOU KNOW?
President Ufifi Bolanga of Bulbosia had a vision in which he saw eight cats, each with one leg and four tails.

Practically **FREE**
Almost **NOTHING TO PAY!**
SHAKESPEARE'S SKULL!

Yes, we have aquired the actual skull of the great bard and are prepared to offer you this fantastic historical curio at rock bottom prices. It's genuine. It's so genuine that you can almost imagine all the noble thoughts that swirled round the premier pen pushers brain as he cooked up all those whacky tales. Send £50 now to receive the genuine skull that once housed the Stratford super-brain. (Or £99 for two).
Special Offer!
For every five skulls you buy we will send you free of charge, the original skull of shakespeare as a boy!

Continuing Horace Toad's amazing revelations of his life as Hollywood's biggest star!

I survived the Gypsy and the mad doctor

During our exclusive series life behind the glamour and glitter of show business, Horace Toad has revealed in intimate detail how he once had a pet canary called Simon, a dog called Rover and a little black cat called Tibbs. Last week he described with agonising frankness the despair and heartbreak he felt when Blaze, his pet goldfish died suddenly in the night. In this issue he tries desperately to make some sense of the shattered remains of his life. Read on . . .

Life has no favourites and Lady Luck respects no man. I knew that now. In the midst of life there is death, and as I clutched the lifeless body of Blaze to my chest – the same chest that had given solace to all the world's leading actresses – I knew I had plunged from a carefree plateau of love and companionship into a soulless void. *Death! Where is thy sting!*

I dropped Blaze lovingly into the waste disposal unit and sat down to ponder the wreckage of my once fun-filled life. As I did so I felt terrible stabbing pains in that part of the anatomy you sit down upon. I leapt gingerly to my feet. What new cruel twist of fate awaited me now?

"Boils."

I looked up to see Clara, my gypsy housemaid standing in the doorway.

"Boils." she repeated. "That's what you've got – boils. It's as plain as the nose on your face. Go and get changed into your robe. There's only one cure for boils."

As if in a dream I wandered upstairs and changed into my silk dressing gown. Clara was right, it was boils. As I changed I heard her downstairs singing a strange gypsy song.

I went down the stairs and saw that Clara was standing by a large tub filled with steaming hot tea leaves.

"This'll soon have you off your feet again." She said, tearing off my robe and pushing me backward into the hot damp leaves. "There's only one cure for boils and that's tea leaves."

Pain seared through my entire body, almost suffocating me. It was excruciating, unbearable. I saw laughter in the evil gypsy's eyes and I knew this was no ordinary cure. With a cry of pain I leapt out from that hellish brew and danced wildly round the room, making John Travolta look like Long John Silver.

Clara's demonic laughter was ringing in my ears as I fled the house in my Rolls Royce. I arrived at my doctor's surgery in a state of some distress. He took me behind some screens and asked me to disrobe. I did so.

"Now bend over."

I did as I was told, anxious for expert medical help to undo the damage. I waited nervously for his verdict.

"Oooooh!" He said. I bit my lip to release the tension.

"My, my, my . . ." he went on, Mmmmm . . . . really!"

I could wait no longer.

"What is it Doctor?" I begged. "What is it? What do you see?"

"I see a tall dark stranger in your life . . ."

OLD! USELESS! EXPENSIVE!

Yes! Yes! YES! Old, useless and expensive items are our forte. We'll give you shoddy goods and make you pay through the nose for them. We have an extensive range of ill-fitting clothes that will make you look and feel so ridiculous you'll want to die. Be an individual! Send us lots and lots of money and if you're lucky we might send you something we can't get rid of anywhere else. Be brave! Stop bowing to convention!

GARDENING CORNER

Well, what a week it's been and no mistake! Greenfly on my nasturtiums, blight on my melons, slugs on my cucumber, large red lumps on my scalp and my radishes have shrivelled away. A not-so-blooming nuisance if you get my meaning.

But, touch wood, not everything in the garden has been so discouraging. My experiments into plants' reaction to stimulae has been going on apace. My banana-fed roses have grown long arms, my milk fed bluebell has started purring and the cactus I watered with whisky has gout and a long red nose. *Important Note.* You'll remember that last week I told you about novel ways of keeping sparrows off the lawn? Well due to a printer's error the last sentence should have read 1 0z of parsnip and *NOT 1,000 tons of gelignite.* Hope none of you were inconvenienced.

I'm staying! Says 'Gibber'

'Gabbling John Gibberish, controversial boss of strife torn Oldcastle Rovers, issued an emphatic denial that he was about to resign following his team's loss of form. Speaking in the dressing room after another lack-lustre display had extended his team's losing run to 509 games The Gibber said forcefully: "No chance. I've got a job to do and I'm going to see it through. All this talk of resignation is just so much hot air."

Asked about his team's performance he continued, "We were robbed. Their twelfth goal was a mile off-side and we should have had a penalty in the first minute when we were only 2-0 down. If we had been given that, it would have changed the picture of the whole game and put us right back in with a chance. The lads sweated blood out there today and I felt for them. The fans have been wonderfully patient as I'm sure they can see what we're trying to do."

Donning a false nose and whiskers and climbing through the window as cries of "Lynch the Gibber!" sounded in the corridor, Gibberish went on: "There's too much nonsense talked about football these days. People take it far too seriously. Football is a business and should be run on the same lines as any other. I use the same principles in a team selection as I did when I was a greengrocer before I came into the game. The tactics are simple – put the big ones at the front and the little ones behind."

Big Shock in Grand National

There was drama at fog-shrouded Aintree last week, when a complete outsider stole Steeplechasing's greatest prize and thousands of angry punters went on the rampage yelling 'fix' and demanding their money back.

The drama centred around Punter's Pal, a nineteen year old mare whose previous best performance was when she went down by a neck to a snail in an all-comers race on Blackpool beach. At the start of the race Punter's Pal looked so fat she could hardly stand up and was quoted at 10,000,000 to 1 by all leading bookmakers. She was left at the start and disappeared into the mist heading for the first fence with some twenty lengths to make up.

What happened next is still the subject of some debate. The thick fog made identifying the runners very difficult but several fancied horses were involved in a melee at Beecher's when an alligator and a gorilla attacked the principal runners. Fans in the grandstand were waiting anxiously for the leaders to appear for the final time when Punter's Pal wandered out of the mist, lay down and gave birth to a foal that cantered across the line. Punters Pal finished second and that grand old battler, the three legged donkey Sportakings was third.

Punter's Pal is owned by Honest Vince DiMaggio, a local bookmaker who had no doubts about the outcome. "I saw it all. The foal deserved to win." Scoffing at suggestions that Punter's Pal had taken a short-cut, Mr. DiMaggio, who also owns a string of pet shops, said "That's what makes racing the colourful sport it is. Punter's Pal jumped like a stag, just like I knew he would. I wouldn't have bet the first three in a forecast if I didn't think she'd got a chance."

DID YOU KNOW?
A pound of chopped liver is heavier in Antarctica than a half pound of sharpened pencils.

DID YOU KNOW?
If you threaten a worm with legal action he will always try and wriggle out of it.

Advertisement

So you couldn't pull out the pull out section eh?

WHAT KIND OF WEAK KNEED SNIVELLING DRIP ARE YOU?

Charles Globe offers you this once in a lifetime chance to have a body just like his.

His *Fantastic Free Offer* gives you cringing repulsive bookworms the chance to be a *Real Man* with gleaming muscles and magnetic charm. His *Amazing New Technique* requires

No Skill
No Excercise
No Intelligence
No Physical Courage
No Willpower

No, you will need none of these demeaning frailties of character to build up your body to Globe size proportions, so what do you say, creep – are you *Man Enough?* Send now for free details.

It was a tough spot all right, and I, Captain Kremmen, the world's most fabulous man, was right in the sticky middle of it all. I'd heard through the cosmic grapevine that the most fiendish minds in the entire universe were planning a pow-wow, and using my initiative, courage, resourcefulness and pocket compass I had found the room they intended to meet in. I'd hardly got inside when I heard them coming, and with only one thin door separating me from them I knew I had to act, and act fast. I went through Hamlet's soliloquy in two seconds flat and then, faster than you could count Tony Blackburn's brain cells, I disguised myself as a two-inch ruler and lay flat across the leather topped desk, waiting for the opening of the door to signify the beginning of . . . .

COUNCIL OF SUPER CRIMINALS

Cosmic crimedom's most notorious duo entered first, the menacing Ryton Brothers. The Ryton Brothers are especially notorious because there's only one of them, and she's a girl. But what a girl! Twelve foot two, fists of blue – against her Superman would stand the same chance as a stuffed rat in the Battersea Dogs' Home. She is deadly, really deadly. At the circus she went straight for the juggler. The last time she was in jail she put a drawing pin on the electric chair. Her last three boyfriends died of colds. A cold isn't usually fatal, but it is when you give it to her.

Hiddy the Freak was the next one in, a four armed deviate from the planet Yekk, with a gruesome face that even as I watched, grew some more. Clock that grisly visage! Natives of Yekk are known for their ugliness, but Hiddy abuses the privilege. As he entered, two mirrors flung themselves to the floor, two chairs scuttled wimpering into the corner and a peeping Tom asked him to draw the curtains. Laso-Fot Image Recorder burst into tears when I took this picture, and it was all I could do to stop myself wriggling in a most un-ruler like manner.

Droid Boy came next, a mechanical delinquent made up entirely of electric toasters, always likely to pop up when there's a chance of burning a crust. He turned to crime after his first owner threw him out for an infra-red griller and now he nurses a pathological hatred for ultra-violent chimpanzees. His criminal prowes is electrifying, his behaviour frequently shocking and his pursuit of all forms of dough relentless. A thinly disguised version of his life can be seen in the film 'Loaf Encounters of A Burnt Kind.'

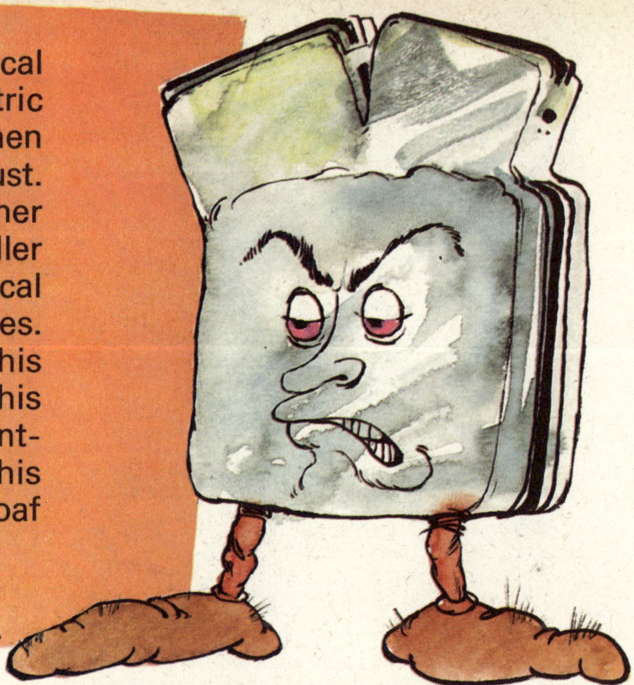

Supermutie slid in close on Droid Boy's heels. After the detergent wars on his home planet Bio-Kleen, it seemed like the end of the line. Everyone had pegged it. They were all washed up. But not so. Out of the foaming, whiter than white slime rose a new breed of supermen, mutated humans totally immune to the effects of soap and water. They had no noses and smelled terribly. Supermutie was the strongest of this new breed and as he entered the room, the plants wilted instantly.

Arwon Dee Jay, or R1 DJ as he is known to his friend, was wheeled in next. This clockwork robot with the ravenous grin painted on his head circuits, is one of the most dangerous objects in the cosmos. Wind him up and his jaw starts moving and sounds that mean death to all that listen issue forth. The grotesque litany uttered through those mechanical lips paralises the body and atrophies the brain. The long lingering death to the accompaniment of a mindless monotonous monologue of gibberish is too fearful to describe here.

Last but not least was Walter Smeem-Weedy from Earth. Walter is an accountant who never pays on buses, drops litter everywhere and once pulled a face at the telly when the Milky Bar Kid was on. His mind has been enfeebled by years of naughty thoughts, but his one burning ambition remains indestructably vibrant and alive – the utter domination of the universe and everything in it.

So there they were, the most vicious gang of sub-human delinquents outside of the House of Commons, and only me to stop them. Luckily, I had snapped them all with my Laso-Fot Image Recorder, and when the meeting was over I slipped back to Earth with my precious evidence.

To this day they have not put their heinous plans into action, but when they do, rest assured that I, Captain Kremmen, the world's most fabulous man, will be ready for them. Forewarned is fore-armed, and although it's a wee bit expensive when it comes to buying gloves, at least we have a chance.

Chill to the four armed invaders!
Thrill to the erupting volcanoes!
Long after Raquel Whoppers!
Lust after Kenny Everett!
Laugh at the high school romps!
Cry for Kiki the kitten.
in the most moving tale ever written of love on the campus in those wild and whacky days of the fun-filled fifties.
C. D. Grifter presents

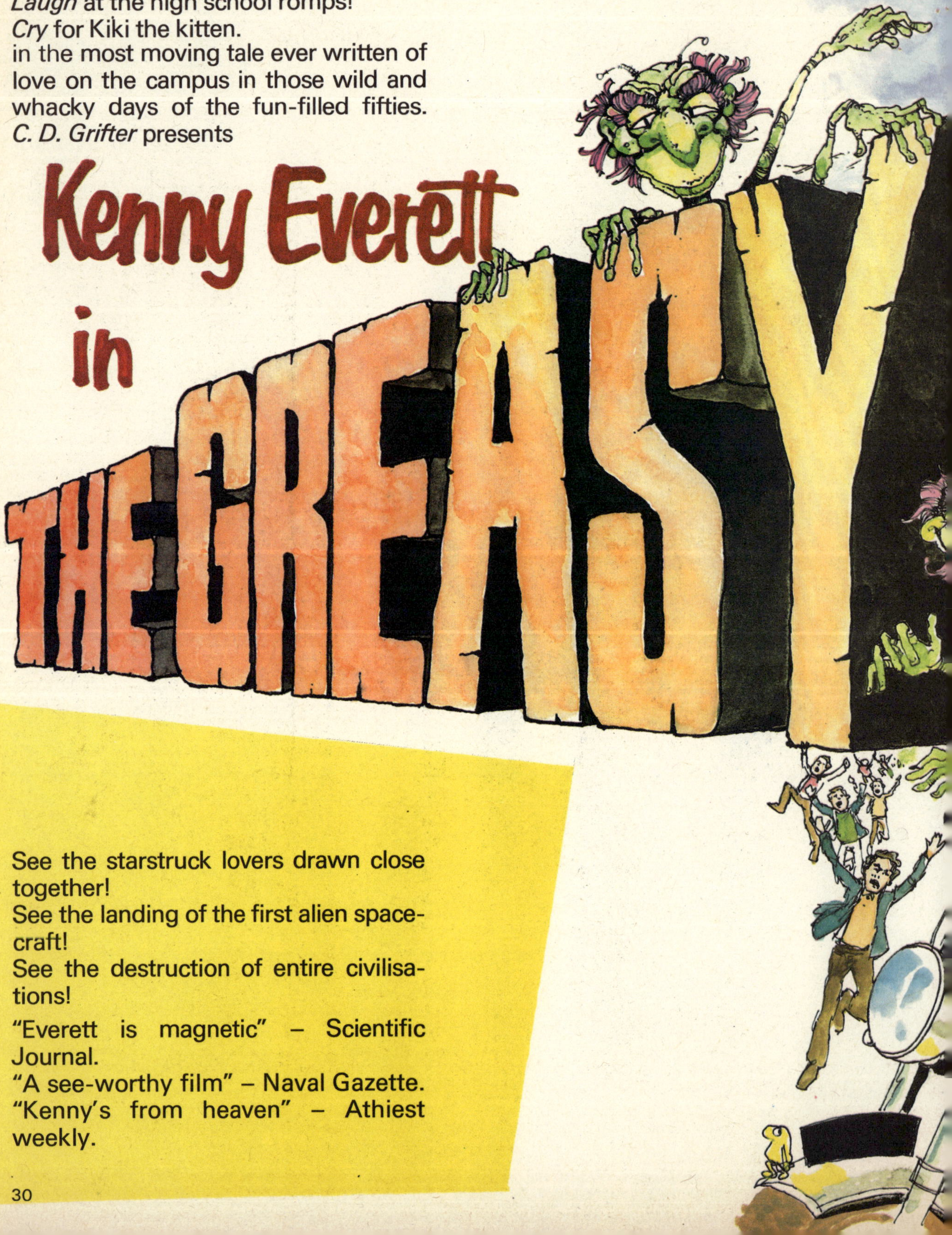

See the starstruck lovers drawn close together!
See the landing of the first alien spacecraft!
See the destruction of entire civilisations!

"Everett is magnetic" – Scientific Journal.
"A see-worthy film" – Naval Gazette.
"Kenny's from heaven" – Athiest weekly.

DEATH! MURDER!
SEX! MADNESS!
DISASTER!
DESTRUCTION!
SONGS GALORE!

HOT
GOSSIP

MADNESS ON PLANET X

Captain Kremmen, Carla and Gitfinger have escaped to planet X with a bunch of Krells in hot pursuit. Little do they know they've stepped out of the frying pay into a terrifying non-world at the crossroads of infinity, where fact and faction are one, where dreams merge with reality, where time and space are not absolute – where relativity is a shimmering mirage and the universe can exist on a speck of dust.

Help them escape from the madness of planet X by playing this game.

A game for two or more players.

Players landing on a square containing a circle must follow the arrow. Players landing on a square containing instructions must obey them. Players landing on a square already occupied by another player must burst into tears. The winner is the first player to reach 100 and stay there.

End of Part One

FREE DAVID COLEMAN'S MOUTH FROM TEN TON CLAMP- GO BACK TO START
ATTACKED BY MAVIS RILEY -GO BACK 20 SPACES
HOT AIR LOSS IN HOUSE OF LORDS- GO FORWARD 5 SPACES
DESTROY A TONY BLACKBURN DUPLICATING MACHINE -GO ON 11 SPACES

Good evening. No, no, don't switch off, I won't hurt you. I'm a doctor. An animal doctor. Do you have any pets? You do? Good, because if you do the chances are that those lovable little tykes are just riddled with fleas. Sorry, but it's true.

Not to worry, I've got a big something just for you. It's right here under the desk, but you can't see it. Sorry, but word gets around you see. Those parasites on your pets . . . They've all heard about it. They've seen it. They know it hurts. They know that if you go out and buy one it'd be curtains for them. Why, if they caught just half a peep of my wondrous product they'd peg it from heart failure. If I even began to describe it half of them would croak themselves on the spot. I can't even give you an address to write to. Before I got past the name of the street those crafty blighters would be off the cat's back and into the fire, and these adverts cost money. I'm helpless. I can't show it to you . . .

Oh go on then –

None rougher, none tougher – Yick just makes us suffer.
Yick is the thing for you-oo-ooooo!

YICK, YICK, YICK, YICK, YICK, YICK, YICK!
Lay it on thick it will do the trick!

Well, actually, I'm sorry to say it isn't isn't Yick is an entirely fictional product. That's why all those fleas are still there. I put it in to test you really. You see, I want to show you my product, I know you want to see it – but if the fleas saw it then they'd be off and your wouldn't need it, so you wouldn't buy it and that's not fair is it? Some of you would have got away scot flea – ha ha – get it? I had thought of writing it backward on the screen so you could hold up a mirror, but the little devils wouldn't fall for that one. As soon as you got up they'd be off to the big doggy in the sky.

No, it's a hopeless situation and they've got us whacked – nudge nudge. The only thing – wink wink – for us humans to do is to give those poor persecuted pests a break. Go on, treat the little monkeys. They deserve it. Get them Fleeglee!

Fleeglee, Fleeglee, Fleeglee's for me
It's just the stuff

If you're feeling rough
Fleeglee's made for every flea!

I was luxuriating in my spacious dressing room listening to five beautiful women begging me to open the door – eventually I had to let them out – when it occurred to me that my wondrousness was not accidental and that at least a small part of it was hereditary, and that I, the apex of the Everett dynasty, might owe something to my distant forebears. I rooted around and lo, I discovered

Fruits on the Family Tree

This is the oldest of all my known relatives. Archaeologists in Kent discovered his petrified remains – mind you I'd be scared myself with all those dinosaurs about. From what we can piece together, he was not a brave man – you can see he had no guts – but he had quite an eye for the ladies. He'd only just come down from the trees but his eyes still swung from limb to limb. I like to think that if he were alive today he'd be very famous – after all he'd be 800,000 years old.

The noble Sir Gawain Everett was one of the finest of my family. He was a knight of the Square Table but kept sitting down with his sword on so they changed the name. It was this great man who advised King John to sign the Magna Carta "As it will all blow over in a couple of weeks." He found the Holy Grail but left it because he didn't want to clutter up the pockets on his armour. He fought in the War of the Roses but was arrested for using insecticides and sentenced to death. His last request to sing 'Twenty Million Green Bottles' was refused and as he laid his noble head on the block his last words were recorded for posterity by the executioner. They were: "I'll get even if it's the last thing I do."

Lady Gwendoline Everett was an eccentric. Well, to be truthful she was more than that. Lady Gwendoline was like Whistler's mother when she stood up – off her rocker. Even as a child she was a little potty and she knew it – she spent most of her time under the bed. She claimed she had to act crazy or she'd go mad. She was superstitious too – she wouldn't work during any week that had a Friday in it. She was committed to an asylum where she spent twenty-five years teaching a spider to yodel. On her release she showed it to the butler. "You see this spider?" she began. The butler hit it with his fist. "I'm sorry, ma'am, I hadn't noticed it before."

Uncle Ebeneezer was the ditherer of the family. He couldn't make his mind up about anything, and as a result he led a varied and interesting life. As a young man he couldn't decide whether to be a hairdresser or a writer. He tossed for it – heads or tales – but the coin landed on it's side so he decided to become an archaeologist. His career was soon in ruins, so he left and set up as a butcher. He couldn't cope with all the chop lifters, so he tried being a tree surgeon but found he couldn't stand the sight of sap. Next he became an inventor and built the world's most efficient mousetrap, but some rat stole it. Finally he hit upon a revolutionary new way of dyeing sheep for identification. His business prospered and he became the biggest lamb dyer in the whole world.

Guzzling Gertie Everett liked a tipple. It all started when her mother put brandy in her milk to keep her quiet when she was a baby. Her first words were "Don't sell that cow." From then on it was one thing after another. If she wasn't beating up half a dozen sailors in a street brawl she was being arrested for speeding in her wheelchair. Eventually she took to staying at home and drinking Mama Rosy's Patent Battling Broth, a strange concoction brewed by the woman in the cellar next door. Her last words were; "I don't know how Rosy can make a profit selling this a tuppence a bottle."

Edmundo Everett was the most artistic member of our family. He had music in his soul – his shoes squeaked. He believed singing was every man's bathright. He practised until he was up to his neck in music playing his own violin. He scraped a living for a while, but after several stage appearances he was forced to retire through illness – the public was sick of him. Broken hearted, he drifted into petty crime. He was always on the fiddle and in the end he got arrested for robbery with violins. On his release he bumped into Yehudi Menuhen. Edmundo was carrying two violins at the time and wanted to show his respect for the great violinist by giving him one of them. "I couldn't make up my mind," he said later. "In the end I kept the old 'un and gave Yehudi my new 'un."

Ethel Everett was not the handsomest of women. Let's face it, she looked worse than a robber's dog. When she was a baby they fed her with a nose-bag. Every time she turned on the telly Angela Rippon dived down behind her desk. Kojak's scalp stood on end. Christopher Lee strangled himself. At Christmas we used to hang her up and kiss the mistletoe. It surprised everyone when she finally got married, but she treated her husband like a god – she was always giving him burnt offerings. He was spellbound by her bird imitations – she ate worms and watched him like a hawk. When she finally died it took the undertaker four months to get her fit for burial.

Luigi Everetti was one of the black sheep huddled round the family tree. While he was still in his cot he tried to carve his name on it, but he was caught by Special Branch. If Luigi's good points were elastic they wouldn't stretch round a flea's knees. People in our town treated him like solid cholera. His mum had to tie a bone round his neck so the dog would play with him. Six watches on either arm and he couldn't tell the time. His face even looked like it had fallen off the back of a lorry, and rolled down a very steep hill. He drank blood from rusty cans and when he was on the run the police searched low and low for him. They finally cornered him in a block of flats with his partner in crime "Restless" Sid Carrion whose name was the nicest thing about him. "What should we do?" asked Sid. "Jump." replied Luigi. "Jump? But we're on the thirteenth floor."

"I'm not superstitious – you go first."

Ernie Everett was another blessed with the Everett looks. As a baby people used to laugh at him and throw nuts at his mother. After one particularly rude little child had peeped into the pram and then fallen writhing on the floor, his mother, the doughty Edwina Everett, who'd had a very bad day at the abbattoir – someone had called her an old cow and she thought they were going to put her down – burst into tears. A kindly gentleman took pity on her plight and asked her if he could do anything. Edwina said she'd love a cup of tea so the man went off to a cafe across the road. When he came back Edwina was still crying. "There, there," he said kindly, "here's your tea, and look – I've brought a nice fresh banana for your pet monkey." As he grew older, Ernie showed he had a flair for finance when he smashed in the head of his piggy bank, and later he developed a very good head for money – there was a slot at the top, and when you turned one of his ears his jaw shot out.

Uncle Collie was a fighting man. As soon as he was old enough he joined the army – he'd always liked boats – and they put him in Intelligence. When war broke out he fought and fought and fought but they still made him go. Once there he showed his mettle, fighting with Monty in Africa and Patton in Europe. They said he was the most argumentative little ratbag they'd ever met. He was always around when the action started though, if not when it finished. He fell at Tobruk, he fell at El Alamein, he fell at Tripoli, he fell at Anzio – he was always blind drunk. His war record was so good that Vera Lynn made a cover version. His most heroic act was when he single handedly saved 2,500 men from almost certain death – he shot the company cook.

Eddie 'biscuit' Everett was a rumour in his own lifetime. He was a man of many parts, all held together by skin. He had a lot of pride and no small amount of sense – he would never stoop to conquer, he'd just get a longer string. He was a physically unappealing man standing 7 feet 3 inches – or he would have done if he'd had his legs straightened; as it was he stood 2 feet 3 inches and he had great difficulty going through doors. He was an expert wrestler of paper bags, was very kind to dried sliced onions, and he once cut a worm in two because he thought it looked lonely.

Ethel Everett was a prodigious eater who could trough with the best. She had racing colours on her knife and fork. Her mouth was a blur. She was onto the pudding before the echo of the soup died down. Despite her prowess she once took half an hour to finish her soup when she went to an outdoor restaurant and it started raining. As a result of her appetite she was rather fat and men showed little interest in her, although Sherpa Tenzing did conquer her north face in 1978. She finally met her first boy-friend when they were both trapped in a revolving door and they have been going around together ever since.

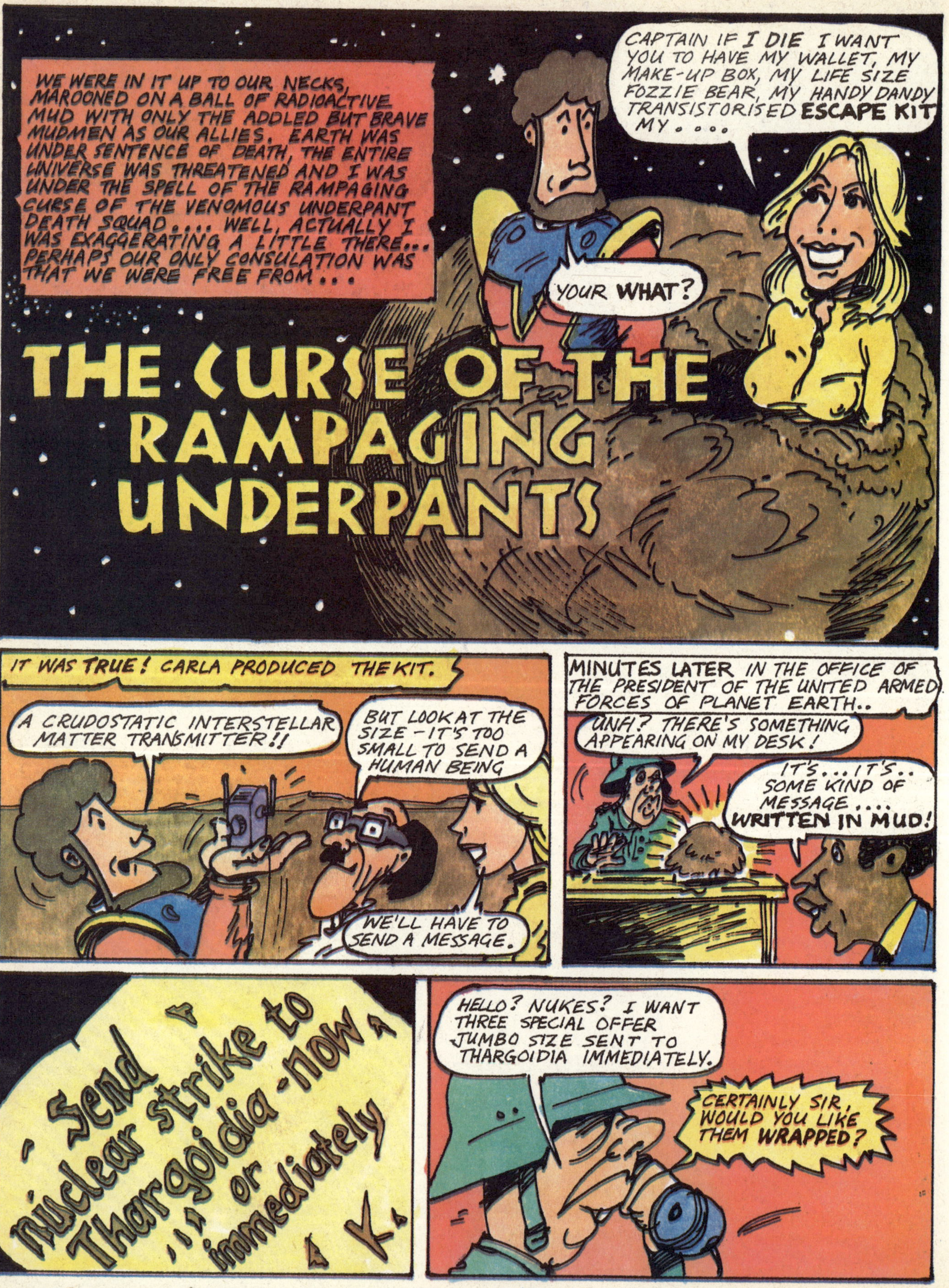
WE WERE IN IT UP TO OUR NECKS, MAROONED ON A BALL OF RADIOACTIVE MUD WITH ONLY THE ADDLED BUT BRAVE MUDMEN AS OUR ALLIES. EARTH WAS UNDER SENTENCE OF DEATH, THE ENTIRE UNIVERSE WAS THREATENED AND I WAS UNDER THE SPELL OF THE RAMPAGING CURSE OF THE VENOMOUS UNDERPANT DEATH SQUAD.... WELL, ACTUALLY I WAS EXAGGERATING A LITTLE THERE... PERHAPS OUR ONLY CONSULATION WAS THAT WE WERE FREE FROM...
CAPTAIN IF I DIE I WANT YOU TO HAVE MY WALLET, MY MAKE-UP BOX, MY LIFE SIZE FOZZIE BEAR, MY HANDY DANDY TRANSISTORISED ESCAPE KIT MY....
YOUR WHAT?
THE CURSE OF THE RAMPAGING UNDERPANTS
IT WAS TRUE! CARLA PRODUCED THE KIT.
A CRUDOSTATIC INTERSTELLAR MATTER TRANSMITTER!!
BUT LOOK AT THE SIZE - IT'S TOO SMALL TO SEND A HUMAN BEING
WE'LL HAVE TO SEND A MESSAGE.
MINUTES LATER IN THE OFFICE OF THE PRESIDENT OF THE UNITED ARMED FORCES OF PLANET EARTH..
UNH? THERE'S SOMETHING APPEARING ON MY DESK!
IT'S...IT'S.. SOME KIND OF MESSAGE.... WRITTEN IN MUD!
Send nuclear strike to Thargoidia - now,,, or immediately
HELLO? NUKES? I WANT THREE SPECIAL OFFER JUMBO SIZE SENT TO THARGOIDIA IMMEDIATELY.
CERTAINLY SIR, WOULD YOU LIKE THEM WRAPPED?

MEANWHILE BACK ON SOONARU 9, A SPACE SHUTTLE HAD LANDED TO COLLECT THE RADIOACTIVE MUD..
ATTENTION YOU SHRIVELLED UP BAGS OF INCONSEQUENCE — BEGIN LOADING THE MUD....
THE GUARD WAS ALONE, BUT HE HAD A GRUNGE GUN. SUDDENLY.....
HERE CAPTAIN TAKE THIS!
I PUT A RADIOACTIVE MUD PIE INTO THE ELASTICATED SUSPENDER AND TOOK AIM...
BULLSEYE! THE MONOPTIC MENACE WAS BLINDED BY THE STINGING SLUDGE..
SPLUDGE
ARGLE
I GRABBED THE DEADLY GRUNGE GUN AND WE MADE READY TO LEAVE ...
CAPTAIN! THE ESCAPE KIT! THERE'S A MESSAGE COMING THROUGH FROM EARTH.
DIT-DIT-DA DIT-DA-DA
WHAT DOES IT SAY?
IT SAYS - DIT-DIT-DA DIT-DA-DA-DIT...
THAT'S MORSE CODE TRANSLATE IT FOR US DOCTOR.
IT'S FROM THE PRESIDENT! HE SAYS HE'S SENT UP A NUCLEAR STRIKE FORCE, BUT THAT WE'RE TO ARREST GORT ANYWAY. JUST TO MAKE SURE.
THAT'S THE PRESIDENT ALL RIGHT. BOY IS HE THOROUGH!
BUT CAPTAIN, IF WE ARE ON THARGOIDIA WHEN THE ATTACK COMES - WONT ALL THE BOMBS LAND ON US?
ULP! YOUR RIGHT!

WAIT - THERE'S MORE! HE SAYS HE KNOWS THIS INVOLVES THE ULTIMATE SACRIFICE BUT HE ALSO KNOWS WE'D BE GLAD OF THIS CHANCE TO DIE FOR HIM..
THE PRESIDENTS BRAVE WORDS SENT LAND-OF-HOPE-AND GLORIOUSNESS WELLING IN MY POCKETS..
HE'S RIGHT! WE DON'T MIND GETTING BLOWN TO BITS DO WE?
WELL, MAYBE JUST AN ITSY BITSY-EENY WEENY-ICKLE BIT.
WE DON'T MIND FOR OURSELVES CAPTAIN, BUT YOU - YOUR SO BRAVE, SO STRONG, SO HANDSOME, SO....
CARLA WAS RIGHT, OF COURSE, BUT SHE WAS SUCH A BRICK I FELT HONOUR BOUND TO GET FRAZZLED TO A CRISP BY HER SIDE.
FORGET ME CARLA, IT'S ALL FOR ONE AND ONE FOR ALL! LETS GO!
WE GATHERED THE MUDMEN WITH US AND SET OFF.
BEFORE LONG WE WERE ORBITING THARGOIDIA,
I CAN'T SEE ANY BOMBS YET.
THARGOIDIA
NOR ME, BUT EITHER LUNCH DIDN'T AGREE WITH ME -OR- I'VE GOT ATOMIC ACHE...
I TOOK HER IN LOW
THERE! THAT'S GORTS PALACE! FASTEN YOUR SEAT BELTS!
NO NEED! I'M GOING TO MAKE ANOTHER SOFT LANDING..
SPLANG
ATROCKLE
WAMCH
Tink

THIS TIME WE WERE READY FOR THEM. I AIMED THE CAPTURED GRUNGE GUN.....
SURRENDER PITIFUL DROPS OF ANAEMIA!
NEVER! TAKE THIS!
GRUNGE SQUINCH IK!!
GOTTERDAMMERUNG! WHAT A WEAPON YOU HAVE, CAPTAIN! THEY'RE ALL INDISPOSED!
RIGHT DOCTOR. NOW WHERE'S GORT'S THRONE-ROOM FROM HERE?
MAYBE IT'S UP THOSE STAIRS, OUT THROUGH THE SECRET COMPARTMENT AT THE BACK OF THE BROOM CUPBOARD, IN THROUGH THE TOILET WINDOW ALONG THE CORRIDOR, DOWN THE CHUTE, ROUND THE ROUNDABOUT, ON THE BUS AND THEN A TAXI THE REST OF THE WAY...
SURE ENOUGH CARLA'S HUNCH WAS CORRECT. SECONDS LATER.
GET GRUNGED GUARDS!
INCHY! OODGE IK!
ONE HEFTY KICK FROM MY MIGHTY BOOT DEMOLISHED THE DOOR
KREMMEN! HOW DARE YOU BURST IN HERE!
I'LL BURST WHERE I LIKE - YOU TIN-POT NEO-NERO.
I'VE ALREADY DESTROYED YOUR PUNY ATTACK FROM EARTH. NOW I WILL DESTROY YOU.
NOT WHILE I BREATH YOU OBNOXIOUS MUCK-BUCKET
SUDDENLY MY ATTENTION WAS DISTRACTED BY AN IMPORTANT RADIO ANNOUCEMENT.
WE HAVE JUST HEARD THAT A ROGUE NEUTRON BOMB HAS GONE OUT OF CONTROL AND THAT THE WHOLE UNIVERSE WILL BE BLOWN OUT OF EXISTENCE IN 2 MINUTES. THE FULL IMPLICATIONS OF THIS WILL BE DISCUSSED IN TONIGHT'S NEWS, BUT ALREADY LADBROKES ARE OFFERING 2-1 THAT THERE WILL BE NO SURVIVORS.

2-1? THAT MEANT IT WAS SERIOUS. SUDDENLY MY LITTLE FEUD WITH GORT SEEMED PETTY....
THE END OF EVERYTHING AS WE KNOW IT CAPTAIN, AS A MAN OF INTEGRITY I KNOW YOU WOULDN'T WANT TO DIE WITH YOUR WEAPON IN YOUR HAND
I DON'T KNOW....
BY MY WATCH THERE'S ONLY ONE MINUTE AND 15 SECONDS LEFT!
75-74-73-72....
GORTY COULD BE RIGHT. WHY SHOULD HE LIE NOW? HE CAN'T BE ALL BAD.
PUT YOUR GUN DOWN CAPTAIN. LETS LEAVE THIS LIFE AS FRIENDS.
OH YES CAPTAIN AND THEN WE CAN SAY GOODBYE PROPERLY.
49-48-47-46....
I PUT MY GUN ON THE TABLE
OH CAPTAIN - THERE'S SO LITTLE TIME - COULDN'T WE...
CARLA OLD STICK- I DON'T WANT TO BE RUDE- BUT YOU'VE PUT YOUR ARM AROUND ME FOUR TIMES NOW
WHAT AN ARM
18-17-16-15-14....
10-9-8-7-6-5-4-3½-3.....
GOODBYE FRIENDS BOTH OLD AND NEW. WE HAVE TASTED LIFE AND EATEN WITH HONOUR. WE HAVE DONE OUR BIT AND NOW ALL THAT'S LEFT IS TO SAY AGAIN, GOODBYE AND MAY WE ALL MEET AGAIN IN HEAVEN. FAREWELL WORLD!
2½-2-1½-1-⅞-⅔-⅝-½-⅜-0!
CAPTAIN-HEAVEN'S JUST LIKE THE ROOM WE WERE STANDING IN.
IT IS THAT ROOM YOU TRUSTING LITTLE TOMATO SEED -STICK 'EM UP!
GOTTERDAMMERUNG!
BY THE BEARD OF MY MOTHER - YOU TREACHEROUS SLOP OF DEPRAVITY.
YOU TRUSTING NURD! I KNEW MY FAKE BROADCAST WOULD FOOL YOU. NOW THAT YOU'VE GOT ALL SENTIMENTAL ABOUT DYING IT'S UNFAIR TO DEPRIVE YOU OF THE PLEASURE.
IT'S FRYING TIME!

WORKING WITH INCREDIBLE SPEED, I UNSCREWED MY BIG TOE....
FASTENED IT ONTO THE THING IN MY POCKET....
MOVE TWO OF THE CLIPS TO THE RIGHT,
TIED ON THE HOOK IN MY TROUSERS, GLUED TOGETHER TWO FIDDLY BITS, - SCREWED IN THAT THING THAT LOOKS LIKE A FLANGE TURNED THE WHOLE THING ON IT'S SIDE, SPAN THE WHEEL, ADDED A DAB OF SPIT TO THE BIT ON THE END AND THEN....
A SPACE CANNON !!!
EXACTLY YOU BACKSLIDING RECIDIVIST! THROW YOUR GUN DOWN.
GORT KNEW WHEN HE WAS BEATEN, HE THREW DOWN HIS GUN.
RIGHT, NOW ALL THAT REMAINS IS TO SET UP A GOVERNMENT OF MUDMEN AND THEN WE CAN TAKE OUR PRISONER BACK TO EARTH.
CAPTAIN YOU'RE WONDERFUL.
EVERYTHING WENT SMOOTHLY - AND SECONDS LATER...
THIS ISLAND EARTH - IT'S A BEAUTIFUL PLACE, ISN'T IT CARLA?
NOT AS BEAUTIFUL AS YOU, CAPTAIN.
WE HANDED GORT OVER TO THE PROPER AUTHORITIES AND THEN WENT TO A SPECIAL PARTY HELD BY THE PRESIDENT HIMSELF....
FOR THEY ARE JOLLY GOOD FELLOWS FOR THEY ARE JOLLY GOOD FELLOWS
CAN'T WE SLIP AWAY FOR A FEW HOURS CAPTAIN? I'VE GOT SOMETHING I JUST KNOW YOU'D LOVE TO PLAY WITH.
YOU DONT MEAN?
YES DARLING YES - YES - YES.
YOUR RUBBER MOUSE THAT REALLY SQUEAKS, EVEN WHEN YOU DON'T TOUCH IT - THE ONE WITH A DIDDLY ON IT'S GLOCKENSPIEL?
DARLING I LOVE YOU!

HOT GOSSIP

KENNY SHUFFLE

Hi there, dance fans! Kenny E's the name and dancing's my game, so hang loose. If you're hot to trot, this is the spot. Get hip to the trip, don't give me the pip and be cool, don't play the fool. We've got a brand new dance you're gonna love to prance, so get hep to the step and shake your booty to those fabulous sounds we're gonna lay on you. Yes *You* baby and big Kenny don't mean maybe!

Now I bet you girls are all a-quiver like a bag full of arrows, waiting for my magnificent body to enthrall that heaving seething mass of humanity on the dance floor, so I'll just finish this bloater paste sandwich then away we go!

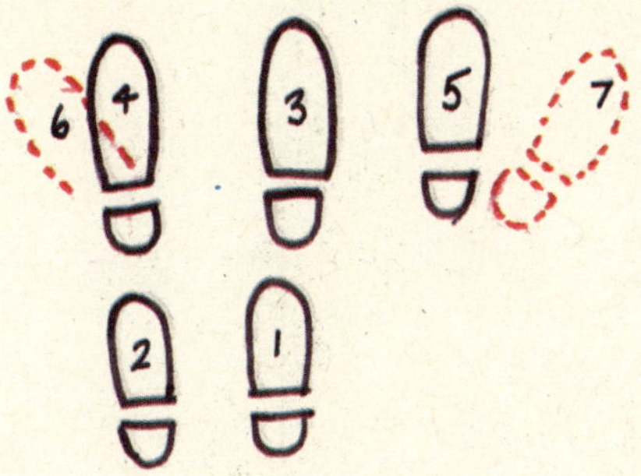

1. Step forward.
2. Step forward (*thrust*).
3. Step aside (*kick, thrust*).
4. Kick, wiggle, wave.
5. Side (*raise arms*).
6. Kick, bend.
7. Stretch, kick.

Shake that thing!

1, 2. Step forward.
3, 4. Point toes inward.
5, 6. Twirl legs inward through 180°.
7. Call ambulance.

Right on, brother!

1. Lose your inhibitions.
2. Wiggle suggestively.
3. Wink lewdly.
4. Leer.
5. Run for it.

School for Devious Humour

It was a tough caper - that's why I was on the job. The evil Scrunges had begun a secret battle to take over the universe and their first target was earth. Computer print-outs had shown that Scrunges have a bland psychological profile, so I figured they had to be getting help from earth men. Their plans were so fiendish, so dastardly in concept that they had to be the work of a fevered earth brain. But who would betray his own planet to the Scrunges? No human would willingly do that, so it had to be that they were being tricked into it.

My investigations led me to the School of Devious Humour and I decided to check it out. I climbed into an air vent and made my way along the shaft until I came to a grille overlooking a room marked Admissions. As the first applicant came in I switched on my super sensitive sonic recorder. This is an exact transcript of the fiendish revelations that followed.

Applicant: Hello, is this where you come to enroll?

Interviewer: Blah blah blah blah blah blah. Blah Blah blah.

A: Unh? . . .

I: Blah blah blah blah blah comfortable.

A: Eh? . . . What? . . . Oh! . . . I see! I get it now. The school for devious humour. Yes, very good. I expect you're a post graduate aren't you. Have you heard the –

I: This is not the school for devious humour.

A: What?

I: This is an army recruitment office – the Scrunge Secret Army.

A: The Scrunge Secret Army? . . . Oh yes, yes, yes – the Scrunge Secret Army. Not the School for devious humour at all, No, nothing to do with it.

I: That's right. Nothing. Do you still want to join?

A: It's been my life's ambition to join the Scrunge Secret Army – after joining the School for devious humour of course. He he.

I: Have you any qualifications?

A: I watch Crossroads every night and I've got a cut-out model of Nicholas Parsons with moveable parts.

I: Are you trying to be funny?

A: No, no, no, no, no, no, no . . . well yes.

I: Well you've failed – pitifully, and that amuses me. Will you care to sign?

At this juncture I switched off the tape, kicked out the grille and lept into the room.

Don't sign that paper!

At the sight of me the Scrunge knew the game was up. As Scrunges do on such occasions, he metamorphosed into a tiny plasticine robot and scurried under the skirting board. I looked at applicant whose smile had left his face.

"It's all right, now son – you can smile if you want."

"Smile? I've never seen anything so stupid in my entire life."

Diaries of the Superstars

In the gruelling and physically exhausting world of the rich, talented and famous, rock stars are subjected to a harrowing schedule of wild parties, hysterical adulation, wild parties, vast amounts of money, luxurious hotels, first class travel, wild parties, naughty women and wild wild parties.

Just as in war a certain camaraderie comes to the fore, so in the white heat of this hell on earth called superstardom, strong, lasting, meaningful friendships are forged. Only last week I saw the beautiful and talented Debbie Harry, and if I hadn't been quick ducking down from the window she'd have seen me too. I consider myself very close to some of the world's biggest stars and have been welcomed into many of their homes, where I invariably tie them to the bannisters, smear jam on their cats, drop stinkbombs in their kitchens and peep at their diaries.

Here are some extracts from those diaries – simple, moving documents chronicling their authors hopes, dreams and ambitions.

First off we take a look at the private diary of reggae superstar I. Rule, whose strict adherence to the religious code of Niddy is in direct contrast to his wild stage act.

I and I-man awoke to another splendid morning granted couteously by my great leader Niddy, King Of Kings, Lion Of Lions, Scourge of Babylon, Mighty Ruler, Most Regal Potentate, Glorious Guru and Extremely reasonably priced Plumber Who Always Shows Up When Called And Once Played Golf With Don Revie The Ex-Manager of England Football Team. In accordance with the strict doctrine of my beliefs I shall not partake of any food that was not served by the woman in the supermarket with the large chest, unless, of course I am some large distance away when mighty hunger strikes. Nor shall I partake of alcoholic beverages of any shape or form unless my mouth gets all dry, and nor shall I dally with temptation in the form of the other sex unless they're real lookers.

In accordance with the true aims of the great leader Niddy, King of Kings, Lion of . . . .

Fascinating stuff, and so's this next one – the diary of rock megastar and extremely concerned individual Rick Macho.

They hate me. All of them. They're all jealous of me, especially my psychiatrist. He won't believe I can't stop telling lies. That Iago of an agent is no better. He won't do anything for me anymore. He won't give me the help I need to make my music. He ad-libbed during my press conference about lack of communication. He's still not set up my round the world solo yacht voyage yet. And if he'd got me a decent accountant in the first place, I wouldn't have to spend twelve million dollars before the end of the tax year. I feel so goldarned plain *Angry* that I might get out of bed today. Or tomorrow. Of course, I'd better check with my astrologer first, but he's been getting at me a bit too lately, so maybe I'd better just throw my gold encrusted runes and if they tell me the vibes are right to get drunk then go down to the recording studios and make rude noises.

Next we have punk rock star Sid Scab, one of the most violently committed men on the music scene today.

Woke up feeling sick and awful. They left. God, how I hate those phoney punks! They're not fit to sniff the saddle on my bike. All that posing and posturing makes them too intelligent to be a real punk like me, who's too ignorant to shrug off the Socio-Political shackles of a materialistic society that bind me to a treadmill, that only Neo-marxism can break when hypocrites like Rod Stewart and Rick Macho who are too old and rich to know anything about the *Real* world, where real punks like me who can't relate to superstars in big mansions with no street-credibility and are too badly educated to channel our aggression and dole queue frustrations into anything other than a violent, naked flame of passionate anger against everyone who oppresses us or looks at us funny in the pub just 'cos I've got a toilet seat round my neck and I'm firing a machine gun.

Gosh, for someone who is a professor at Cambridge, Sid's quite a live wire, which is more than can be said for our last tragic diarist, the late, great Hartlepool Blues singer who inspired every major change in rock from Sinatra to Dylan to Lennon to Des O'Connor – that unsung hero of acoustic grit, Deaf Joe Higginbottom. These are the very last entries in Joe's diary.

Monday.
Woke up this morning . . . Thanked the stars I was alive.
Tuesday.
Woke up this morning . . . Thanked the stars I was alive.
Wednesday.
Didn't wake up this morning . . . Damn these stars, I must have died.

GET AWAY FROM IT ALL... IN GRENUSIA

Where do superheroes go to super-relax? Where can cosmic royalty canoodle away from prying eyes? What is the number one resort for extremely rich people?

Mars? Venus? Sticklebania? Huddersfield? The kitchen?

No, the place everyone's talking about is Grenusia, the now place for tomorrow's people soon, and this exotic location still has an extremely limited number of vacancies for a once in a lifetime holiday. We here at Paltrifun Tours can offer you a fabulous weekend on the unspoiled hideaway of Grenusia for just six billion galactic scroats and three labels from a glass of water.

"How will I get there?" you may ask. Well. you'll get there the only way Paltrifun Tours knows how – *In Style!*

Chariot Of The Nobs

You will be travelling in this magnificent spacecraft, the S.S. Burstinto Flame, which has been especially shaved and deodorised under each wing. The walls of the spacious interior are hung with many old masters, including some of Rembrandt's extremely rare felt tip studies. Your 29 year outward journey will be further enlivened by a loop tape of Max Bygraves singing 'Deck of Cards' and a continuous video tape of Frank Carson laughing.

The Flat Mountains

The flat mountains are one of nature's most fascinating creations. Lying completely flat, these grey coloured behemoths stretch as far as the eye can see, and are extremely easy to climb.

The Stick

This famous landmark, a six-inch splinter from a packing crate, is the cornerstone of one of Grenusia's most fabulous mysteries. Scientists believe that the stick is absolute proof that in the far distant past, Grenusia was invaded by alien beings of vastly superior intelligence who brought the stick with them to prod the little puddles of Grenusians.

Fun Person
Sheila Shuttlemuck, your efficient hostess, may not be beautiful, but she's a *Fun Person* and she's got plenty of whacky japes up her voluminous sleeves to keep everybody laughing and promote a real family feeling. If you find salt in your tea, a jar full of poisonous space rats ties to your face or molten lava in your underclothes don't worry – it's all just a giggle, and Sheila will be going out of her way to shorten the faces of any killjoys or stick-in-the-muds you might have aboard. Sheila's busy schedule leaves her little time for personal hygiene, and passengers are advised that gas masks and barge-poles are available under the seat at very reasonable prices.

Getting excited all ready? Well, hold onto your heart because there's more!

Captain Courageous
Your pilot for your amazing journey to happiness will be Space Ace Dropsy O'Dither who you can tell is top drawer because he removes the price labels from his bottles, drinks from a glass, and his tattoos are only marginally mis-spelt. The pock marks on his face are not rice scars from his twelve marriages nor the result of some easily transmissable exotic disease. They are the scars of battle, a tribute to Dropsy's perseverance and our exemplary Pilot Training Scheme, where the brave skipper spent nine years mastering the use of a fork.

For those of you who are travelling to Grenusia for the first time, we have included some hints and useful phrases that will make your trip that much more satisfying.

First of all, tipping. Tipping is optional of course, but some of you might like to show willing, so we've included a list to be used as a general rule of thumb.

Hover Taxis	1 dustbin lid per inch travelled.
Waiters	1 quick squirt of insecticide.
Porters	1 extremely hard blow with a hammer.
Bell-Boys	1 wry grin.

As misunderstanding simple conversations is held by the Grenusians to be the most unforgiveable social sin, it might be prudent to learn some everyday terms. A short glossary is included below.

Grenusian-English

Iggy wiggy diggy liggy bang ting pop schlugenbackerwalrus .... Yes.
Iggy wiggy diggy liggy bang ting pop schlurgenbackerwalruss .... No.
Iggy wiggy diggy liggy bang ting pop schlurgenbackerwalrusss .... Perhaps.
Iggy wiggy diggy liggy bang ting pop schlurgenbackerwalrussss Definitely.

English-Grenusian

Hello .... Good riddance and don't come back.
Goodbye .... Hello.
My auntie's pen is full of water .... nininininiwhockle.
The outrage is in my pocket .... nininininiwhackle.
The eels have eaten the seaweed .... nininininiwhickle.
Please don't hurt me, please please .... nininininiwheckle.
Just you try it, sludge-bucket .... nininininiwhuckle.

There, now everything's clear. All you've got to do is come along.

Have A Nice Holiday!

Late News

Good evening.

The Royal doctor today announced that Princess Anne has fully recovered from her back injury and is now able to climb the stairs at her home. The Princess said "That's a relief. I'm sick of climbing that drainpipe."

After complaints that their meals were getting smaller and smaller, canteen manager at the Woofit Down Food Emporium, Mr Ernest Deadly, said: "Nonsense. The meals are the same size as they ever were. It's just that the new wallpaper makes the rooms look bigger."

A pet shop owner was fined today for refusing to wear a crash helmet. The Tortoise he had strapped to his head was ruled insufficient protection.

The Great Cyrano, a circus act appearing under the billing 'Twelve budgies at attention on one nose' appeared in court for an offence under the Trades Description Act when it was discovered that the one on the end had to stand on one leg.

Scottish Scientists today claimed to have developed a revolutionary new hearing aid consisting of a piece of string that is dangled from the ear. It doesn't improve the hearing, but everyone talks louder.

An elderly man was today recovering after being attacked by a pair of shoes. He soon polished them off.

An actor who was given the important part of Frankenstein, yesterday gave it back and apologised, saying he didn't know it had been stolen.

An independent television company has crossed William Hickey with a hot cross bun in an effort to get the ultimate expert on current affairs.

A nuclear power worker was taken to hospital today after swallowing a small piece of uranium. Doctors said he had severe atomic ache.

Defending government policies after securing another massive loan from the IMF the Prime Minister said in Parliament: "I've always wanted to be rich enough to be eccentric."

And now for the weather.

There will be frogs in hilly areas and eels on high ground.

Later, low flying clouds of Bernard Manning masks will be coming in from the west, causing deep depression, and Raquel Whoppers will have a very cold front.

Amazingly accurate weather predictions say there will be severe storms towards the last pages of the Kenny Everett Video Show Annual with plenty of thunder and occasional flashes of –

KODAK SAFETY FILM 5077
KODAK SAFETY FILM 5036
WHO DO YOU
TOWN HALL
THAMES